THE ECONOMIC OUTLOOK FOR THE NATION

WEDNESDAY, JANUARY 25, 1995

U.S. SENATE,
COMMITTEE ON FINANCE,
Washington, DC.

The hearing was convened, pursuant to recess, at 10:00 a.m., in room SD–215, Dirksen Senate Office Building, Hon. Bob Packwood (chairman of the committee) presiding.

Also present: Senators Moynihan, Baucus, Bradley, Pryor, Rockefeller, Conrad, Graham, Moseley-Braun, Chafee, Grassley, Pressler, D'Amato, and Murkowski.

OPENING STATEMENT OF HON. BOB PACKWOOD, A U.S. SENATOR FROM OREGON, CHAIRMAN, COMMITTEE ON FINANCE

The CHAIRMAN. The committee will come to order. Good morning, Dr. Greenspan.

Dr. GREENSPAN. Good morning.

The CHAIRMAN. We are delighted to have you with us.

Normally I try to encourage the members to make short opening statements. My feeling is that some may have a few statements to make before you talk.

I would simply say this. I have listened to you testify, I suppose, 15 times over the years. I agree with your theme of the deficit and the theme of savings. I think it simply becomes more imperative each year because each year that we postpone it, each year that we do not do it, we are living longer and longer on borrowed ideas, borrowed money, and borrowed time. We cannot do that forever. I appreciate what you have said in the past and

I look forward to what you have to say today.

Senator Moynihan?

Senator MOYNIHAN. I would simply repeat exactly what you said and say the same thing.

Welcome, sir.

Dr. GREENSPAN. Thank you.

The CHAIRMAN. Senator Grassley.

Senator GRASSLEY. You do not want opening statements?

The CHAIRMAN. Preferably not.

Senator GRASSLEY. But we can give them if we want to?

The CHAIRMAN. That is correct.

Senator GRASSLEY. I will be prepared next time.

The CHAIRMAN. All right.

Senator Baucus?

Senator BAUCUS. Thank you, Mr. Chairman. I do have some comments I want to make, but I will wait until questions before making them.

The CHAIRMAN. Senator Chafee.

Senator CHAFEE. I have no statement. Thank you. I am glad to see Dr. Greenspan.

The CHAIRMAN. Senator Rockefeller.

Senator ROCKEFELLER. I will wait to hear the witness, Mr. Chairman.

The CHAIRMAN. Senator Conrad.

Senator CONRAD. I will be glad to withhold as well.

The CHAIRMAN. Senator Murkowski.

Senator MURKOWSKI. In that spirit, I am interested in collateral.

The CHAIRMAN. Senator Bradley.

Senator BRADLEY. Mr. Chairman, I have a lengthy opening statement. But I gather from the stares of everyone, including the Chairman, it would be unwise to proceed, so I will not proceed.

The CHAIRMAN. I appreciate the forbearance of all the members.

Dr. Greenspan?

STATEMENT OF HON. ALAN GREENSPAN, CHAIRMAN OF THE BOARD OF GOVERNORS OF THE FEDERAL RESERVE SYSTEM

Dr. GREENSPAN. Thank you very much, Mr. Chairman. I am delighted to be here. I would express my congratulations to you, Mr. Chairman, on becoming, again, Chairman of this committee.

I am pleased, as always, to be able to appear before this committee to offer my thoughts on the economic backdrop of your policy discussions.

The American economy has recorded some notable achievements over the past few years, but there is, nonetheless, much left to be accomplished. Fiscal decisions made by the Congress in the next several months will play a critical role in determining the economic welfare of our citizens over the years—indeed, the decades—to come.

I, perhaps, should begin with a brief review of the current condition of the economy. There is no question that the past year was one of remarkable progress along many dimensions of macroeconomic performance.

The official estimates for the fourth quarter are not yet available, but it is clear that real gross domestic product expanded by about four percent over the course of 1994, the best gain in some time, and one that surpassed most expectations.

Importantly, we saw an accelerated expansion of employment as well. Cumulatively, payrolls have now increased roughly six million over the past couple of years, belying in dramatic fashion the notion that had developed in this decade that our economy had lost its job-generating ability.

With the rapid growth of employment, the national unemployment rate has fallen sharply, to less than 5.5 percent this past month. The economic gains have clearly been broad. They have encompassed almost all major segments of industry in all parts of the country.

The expansion in recent quarters has been paced by growth of business investment and exports and, as a consequence, we have

S. HRG. 104–3

THE ECONOMIC OUTLOOK FOR THE NATION

HEARING

BEFORE THE

COMMITTEE ON FINANCE
UNITED STATES SENATE

ONE HUNDRED FOURTH CONGRESS

FIRST SESSION

JANUARY 25, 1995

Printed for the use of the Committee on Finance

U.S. GOVERNMENT PRINTING OFFICE
88–545—CC WASHINGTON : 1995

For sale by the U.S. Government Printing Office
Superintendent of Documents, Congressional Sales Office, Washington, DC 20402
ISBN 0-16-046917-1

COMMITTEE ON FINANCE

BOB PACKWOOD, Oregon, *Chairman*

BOB DOLE, Kansas
WILLIAM V. ROTH, JR., Delaware
JOHN H. CHAFEE, Rhode Island
CHARLES E. GRASSLEY, Iowa
ORRIN G. HATCH, Utah
ALAN K. SIMPSON, Wyoming
LARRY PRESSLER, South Dakota
ALFONSE M. D'AMATO, New York
FRANK H. MURKOWSKI, Alaska
DON NICKLES, Oklahoma

DANIEL PATRICK MOYNIHAN, New York
MAX BAUCUS, Montana
BILL BRADLEY, New Jersey
DAVID PRYOR, Arkansas
JOHN D. ROCKEFELLER IV, West Virginia
JOHN BREAUX, Louisiana
KENT CONRAD, North Dakota
BOB GRAHAM, Florida
CAROL MOSELEY-BRAUN, Illinois

LINDY L. PAULL, *Staff Director and Chief Counsel*
LAWRENCE O'DONNELL, JR., *Minority Staff Director*

CONTENTS

OPENING STATEMENT

AGENCY WITNESS

seen not only a continuation of robust increases in service sector employment, but also a significant upturn in job creation in the manufacturing sector.

Manufacturing output increased 6.8 percent last year and measured factory employment rose almost 300,000. I say "measured" because it has been true for some time now that manufacturers have relied, to an increasing degree, on workers supplied by temporary help firms, which are recorded separately in the service industry.

But it is clear that last year saw a significant gain in the overall factory work force. Moreover, I would note the reports in the recent Federal Reserve survey, the so-called "Beige Book" assembled by our regional Reserve Banks, that manufacturers now are expressing a greater inclination to add workers directly to their payrolls.

This is a sign of the greater confidence that firms now have that future levels of activity will remain high.

Geographically, contractions in some sectors such as defense and finance have left their negative imprints on certain locales, but rising activity and improving job opportunities have characterized most areas of the country.

Notably, California—accounting for roughly an eighth of the Nation's economy—appears to be in the process of turning around. Unemployment rates have fallen in all regions and are lower in most now than they were at the peak of the last business cycle expansion. Moreover, the gains in employment have benefitted all major demographic segments of the labor force as well.

Of crucial importance to the sustainability of these gains, they have been achieved without a deterioration in the overall inflation rate. The Consumer Price Index rose 2.7 percent last year, the same as in 1993. Inflation at the retail level, as measured by the CPI, has been a bit less than 3 percent for 3 years running now, the first time that has occurred since the early 1960's.

This is a signal accomplishment, for it marks a move toward a more stable economic environment where households, businesses, and governmental units can plan with greater confidence and operate with greater efficiency. When we consider the probable upward bias of the CPI, it would appear that we have gotten close to achieving effective price stability, though we are not there yet.

In 1994, we had a difficult reversal in monetary policy to navigate. The overhang of debt and the strains that emerged among our financial intermediaries, especially out of the commercial real estate collapse of the late 1980's, required a heavy dose of monetary ease beginning in 1989 to alleviate a significant credit crunch.

The danger of overstaying that policy of ease was clear, particularly as we moved through 1993, but the right time to change course was difficult to determine. Judging from the developments of the past year, it appears that our policy reversal last February was timely, but we will not know for sure except in retrospect.

Mr. Chairman, as I have stated many times in Congressional testimony, I firmly believe that a key ingredient in achieving the highest possible levels of productivity, real incomes, and living standards, is the achievement of price stability.

Thus, I see it as crucial that we extend the recent trend of low and, hopefully, declining inflation in the years ahead. The prospects in this regard are fundamentally good, but there are reasons for some concern, at least with respect to the nearer term.

Those concerns relate primarily to the fact that resource utilization rates already have risen to high levels by recent historical standards. The current unemployment rate, for example, is comparable to the average of the late 1980's, when wages and prices accelerated appreciably. The same is true of the capacity utilization rate in the industrial sector.

Clearly, one factor in judging inflationary risks in the economy is the potential for expansion of our productive capacity. If so called potential gross domestic product is growing rapidly, actual output can also continue to grow rapidly without intensifying pressures on resources.

In this regard, many commentators, myself included, have remarked that there is something of a more-than-cyclical character to the evident improvement of America's competitive capabilities in recent years. Our dominance in computer software, for example, has moved us back to a position of clear leadership in advanced technology after some faltering in the 1970's.

But, while most analysts have increased their estimates of America's long-term productivity growth, it is still too soon to judge whether that improvement is a few tenths of a percentage point annually, or even more, perhaps moving us much closer to the more vibrant pace that characterized the early post-World War II period.

It is fair to note, however, that the fact that labor and factory utilization rates have risen as much as they have in the past year or so does argue that the rate of increase in potential is appreciably below the four percent growth rate of 1994.

Mr. Chairman, knowing in advance our true growth potential, obviously would be useful in setting policy because history tells us that economies that strain labor force and capital stock limits tend to engender inflationary instabilities which undermine growth.

Moreover, in such an environment asset prices can begin to rise unsustainably, contributing to an unstable financial and economic environment.

It is true, however, that in modern economies output levels may not be so rigidly constrained in the short run as they used to be when the large segments of output were governed by facilities such as the old open hearth steel furnaces that had rated capacities that could not be exceed for long without breakdown.

Rather, the appropriate analogy today is a flexible ceiling that can be stretched when pressed, but as the degree of pressure increases, the extent of flexibility diminishes.

It is possible for the economy to exceed so called "potential" for a time without adverse consequences by extending work hours, by deferring maintenance, and by foregoing longer term projects.

Moreover, as world trade expands, access to foreign sources of supply augments to a degree the flexibility of domestic productive facilities for goods and some services.

Aggregate indicators, such as the unemployment rate and capacity utilization, may be suggestive of emerging inflation and asset price instability problems. But, they cannot be determinative. History shows clearly that given levels of resource utilization can be associated with a wide range of inflation rates.

Accordingly, policy makers must monitor developments on an ongoing basis to gauge when economic potential is actually beginning to become strained, irrespective of where current unemployment rates or capacity utilization rates may lie.

If we are endeavoring to fend off instability before it becomes debilitating to economic growth, direct evidence of the emerging process is essential. Consequently, one must look beyond broad indicators to gauge the inflationary tendencies in the economy.

In this context, aggregate measures of pressure in labor and product markets do seem to be validated by finer statistical and anecdotal indicators of tensions. In the manufacturing sector, for example, purchasing managers report slower supplier deliveries and increasing shortages of materials.

Indeed, firms appear to have been building their inventories of materials in recent months so as to ensure that they will have adequate supplies on hand to meet their production schedules. These pressures have been mirrored in a sharp rise over the past year in the prices of raw materials and intermediate components.

There are increasing reports that firms are considering marking up the prices of final goods to offset those increased costs. In the labor market, anecdotal reports of shortages of workers have become more common—as indicated, for example, in our Beige Book last week—and there are vague signs of upward pressures on wages.

To be sure, increased wages are a good thing if they can be achieved without commensurate acceleration in prices, but they are not beneficial if they are merely a part of a general pickup in inflation.

A hopeful sign in this regard, however, is that to date the trends in money and credit expansion have remained subdued. They do not suggest that what I have referred to elsewhere as the "financial tinder" needed to support ongoing inflation processes is in place.

That kind of ongoing process also would be expected to involve a different expectational climate than seems to prevail today. Despite the marked improvement in consumer confidence overall, the survey readings on consumers' views of whether jobs are easy to get fall far short of the previous cyclical peak in 1989.

Moreover, there is evidence that the number of people voluntarily leaving their jobs is subnormal currently.

This suggests that the deep-seated fear of job insecurity has not fully dissipated despite ample evidence of strong job growth recently.

Some analysts attribute this phenomenon to workers' concerns about losing health insurance and, for some, pension coverage if they change jobs. Whatever the cause, a lingering sense of insecurity doubtless has been a factor damping wage growth and overall labor costs.

Since the latter, on a consolidated basis, accounts for roughly two-thirds of overall costs in our economy, slower wage growth combined with strong cyclical productivity growth has restrained increases in unit labor costs and hence in prices of final goods and services.

However, as overall output growth of necessity slows in an environment of high resource utilization, so will cyclical productivity growth.

Moreover, if market tightness assuages fears of job insecurity, pressures to raise wages will intensity and unit labor costs could accelerate. In the later stages of previous business cycles profit margins were squeezed, but some of the underlying unit labor cost increases were nonetheless passed through into final goods prices, and inflation picked up.

Thus far in the current cycle, any tendency toward the emergence of this kind of process has been muted by a prevailing concern among firms that, despite capacity pressures, enough slack and subdued unit costs remain in the system to foster competitive inroads on those who try to price above the market.

But this form of discipline may also become less effective as pressures on resources persist. Consequently, it may be that these pressures will lead to some deterioration in the price picture in the near term, but any such deterioration should be contained if the Federal Reserve remains vigilant.

The actions of the Congress and the administration in the fiscal sphere will also be important in maintaining public confidence that inflation will be subdued. There can be no doubt that the persistence of large Federal budget deficits represents in the minds of many individuals a potential risk. While we clearly have avoided it in recent years, history is replete with examples of fiscal pressures leading to monetary excesses and then to greater inflation.

Currently, I strongly suspect that investors here and abroad are exacting from issuers of dollar-denominated debt an extra inflation risk premium that reflects not their estimate of the most likely rate of price level increase over the life of the obligation, but the possibility that it could prove to be significantly greater.

This inflation premium is costly because it raises a hurdle that must be surpassed when looking at the expected returns of possible investment projects.

But the influence of the fiscal imbalance of the Federal Government on capital formation is broader than that. The Federal deficit drains off a large share of a regrettably small pool of domestic private saving, thus contributing further, and perhaps to an even greater degree, to the elevation of real rates of interest in the American economy.

Admittedly, there is some uncertainty about the causes of what seem to be relatively high real long-term rates around the world, as was noted by leaders of the largest industrial nations at their summit meeting last year.

The vast majority of analysts would agree that in the United States the current sizable Federal deficits and the projected growth of those deficits over the decades ahead are a significant element in the story.

In sum, the recent performance of the macroeconomy has been encouraging. But much of the improvement is in the nature of cyclical developments and we all have our work cut out for us if we are to extend these gains and foster long-term trends that enhance the welfare of our citizens.

The central role of the Federal Reserve today is to ensure that our economy remains on a sustainable, non-inflationary path.

For the Congress, a crucial focus should be continuing the process of fiscal consolidation and rectifying the secular shortfall in domestic savings that is limiting the growth of our Nation's productive potential.

Thank you very much, Mr. Chairman.

The CHAIRMAN. Dr. Greenspan, thank you.

The early bird list is as follows. I was here first. Senators Moynihan, Grassley, Baucus, Chafee, Rockefeller, Conrad, Murkowski, Bradley, Graham, D'Amato, and Moseley-Braun.

Dr. Greenspan, in my first 12 years here, my first two terms, I did not support a Balanced Budget Amendment. I was convinced that we would come to our senses and that we had the will, the courage, the capacity, or call it what you want, to narrow the deficits when they were relatively modest in comparison to what they are now.

By 1981 or 1982, I had come to the conclusion we were not going to do it until we were compelled. The pressures to spend in the aggregate were harder to resist than the pressures to save in the specific, and you say you have to save in the specific.

I expect the Balanced Budget Amendment is going to pass, and I think the States are going to ratify it more quickly than we think. I think by the end of our fiscal year this year it is going to be in place and we will be looking at, how do we get to a balance by the year 2002, 2001, or 2003, whatever the time period is we have in the amendment.

There are only three ways to get there. One, of course, is tax increases. I do not know what his present position is, but that is why Milton Friedman used to oppose a Balanced Budget Amendment. He thought we would get there by raising taxes and between the two, he preferred borrowing to taxes because he said at least borrowing is voluntary.

I do not think this Congress or this President would be in the mood to get there by taxes, so that brings us to spending restraints. I will not necessarily say spending cuts, but slowing down the growth of spending so that the spending rises slower than our increase in the revenues and we could balance the budget that way. But then you come to the spending side, and there is really only two large categories. One, is entitlements, and the other, is gifts, grants, call it what you want, to the States.

We have 410 entitlement programs. The bottom 400 cost, plus or minus, about $50 billion. The top four, Medicare, Medicaid, Social Security and other retirement, plus interest, are $900 billion. You could get rid of all 400 and the rest of them go up more in a year than the total that the 400 cost. The entitlement programs, in most cases, the big ones, have index features in them.

If we do not make major restraints in the entitlement programs and we are going to attempt to balance the budget, then I think we look at the $220 billion we give to the States for airports, highways, Medicaid, education, welfare, and everything else, and say that is the only other place from which it could come.

A big factor in our thinking is the Consumer Price Index. I notice you just, in one very nice sentence, kind of breezed by that on something that you said a few days or weeks ago and has caused an immense stir. When we consider the probably upward bias of the CPI—it would appear we have gotten close, and whatnot—could you expand a bit on your view of the CPI and the Federal

Reserve's estimate that it is, as I recall, you said high by a 1–1.5 percent.

Dr. GREENSPAN. Half a percent to 1.5 percent.

The CHAIRMAN. Half a percent to 1.5 percent. Because even if you took the average at one, it is an immense difference, both in what we pay out and in revenues that we have coming in. So I would appreciate if you could expand on that.

Dr. GREENSPAN. Mr. Chairman, I have been aware over the years, as I think virtually every economist has been, that the CPI, by the nature of its construction, overestimates the true cost of living however we wish to define that particular term.

I was particularly impressed by a calculation we made internally which I presented to a joint hearing of the Budget Committees of both Houses, in which we tried to estimate what the effect of the CPI would have been had we not made what, in retrospect, was clearly a most inappropriate set of calculations before 1983 in which we mis-estimated the way in which housing occupancy costs should be factored into the price index.

The Bureau of Labor Statistics has created an index prior to 1983 which replicates the current procedures. So we recalculated what would have happened to the budget deficit currently had the new procedures been in place earlier, and that turns out to be more than $50 billion in fiscal 1994. That is, the budget deficit would have been $55 billion less, as I recall, had the current procedure been in place back then.

That led me to take a closer look at what the impact would be of this clearly general overestimate. If small changes in the CPI can have such an extraordinary effect historically, we should look at what the impact would be in the future if, for example, we took the average of what we expect the over estimate to be—meaning about 1 percentage point—and just formally did the calculation. And, as I indicated to the committees the other day, our estimate is that you save approximately $50 billion in deficits 5 years from now and, cumulatively, approximately $150 billion.

The CHAIRMAN. Over the 5 years.

Dr. GREENSPAN. Over the 5-year period.

The CHAIRMAN. Building up slower to start, to slightly

Dr. GREENSPAN. Correct. And if one wishes to extrapolate it, obviously it gets larger as we move out.

The CHAIRMAN. Senator Moynihan.

Senator MOYNIHAN. I am sure we will want to turn to that subject, Mr. Chairman. But, if I may, just to touch on a matter that I know has concerned the Chairman and the President mentioned last night, and that is the situation of the Mexican economy and the value of that currency.

In your testimony you carefully, consistently, and persistently spoke about pressures on resources and inflationary risk premiums and an economy which has high levels of employment, utilization, and such.

Yet, could I ask your view, it could be that we face an economic crisis in Mexico which could have very large consequences in this country, as I understand, in just the opposite direction, the dropping of demand, dropping of employment, and such. The administration is going to propose a loan guarantee arrangement with the Mexican Government.

I gather they have a practice of selling about $400 billion worth of Treasury bonds, tesobonos, each week.

Yesterday, only $275 million were subscribed at a 25-percent interest rate, which argues a lack of confidence that imperils a great deal of our present arrangements.

Would you speak to that matter and not listen to me?

Dr. GREENSPAN. Well, Senator, I just came from a hearing at the House Banking Committee in which the Secretary of the Treasury, Secretary of State, and myself gave prepared testimony with respect to the Mexican situation.

The general thrust of our remarks was that, with the extraordinary changes that are occurring in the international financial system which has had extraordinarily positive benefits to world economic growth and the underlying standards of living, you nonetheless have got the problem that the huge amount of flow of so-called portfolio capital across borders will, if there are policy mistakes in a major country, cause the reactions in the markets that are very severe.

Indeed, what has happened to Mexico is that, after following an extraordinarily progressive policy for a number of years which brought the Mexican economy from a highly restrictive, government-directed, hyperinflation system to an open market, privatized, price decontrolled system, the Mexican Government, starting about a year ago, began to make a series of mistakes, in part, the result of non-economic forces such as the consequence of the Chiapas rebellion, the political assassination, and the August elections.

As a consequence of that, the huge flow of capital—mainly portfolio capital—which was moving into Mexico, in a sense, as a reward for its extraordinary improvement, began to slow down and then to move out.

Senator MOYNIHAN. By portfolio capital, you would refer to mutual funds.

Dr. GREENSPAN. Stocks, bonds, mutual funds. Exactly.

The Mexican Government, as best I can judge, assumed that the problems were temporary and that after the election, restoration of private confidence and the restoration of capital inflows from abroad would have continued. They were mistaken; it did not.

The result was, having drawn down their reserve balances and issued volumes of these tesobonos to carry them through this period of uncertainty, they found themselves in very dire, short-term financial straits.

It was not a fundamental economic problem, it was the fact that the ability to sustain the foreign capital inflows had temporarily collapsed. And, in today's world, Mexico became the first casualty, if I may put it that way, of the new international financial system.

It is our judgment that there are no simple solutions to this. And, as I indicated in my testimony before the House Banking Committee, I stipulated that I thought that the loan guarantee program which the administration is putting forward is the least worst of a whole series of alternatives.

Loan guarantees are not a good idea. They have lots of problems associated with them. In a sense, they create the wrong incentives. They do not work in a market system.

But, if we have the appropriate type of conditionality, we can eliminate some of the adverse effects. And, in my judgment, the necessity to make certain that the current troubles in Mexico do not spill over into a major crisis beyond the borders of Mexico, requires us to act as best we can to staunch this short-term liquidity problem.

I, frankly, cannot think of anything better than the loan guarantees, which will solve the problem. I have looked at an awful lot of other alternatives. I wish some of them would work, but I cannot honestly say that I have come to any conclusion that there is something easier to do that will work than the particular set of guaranty programs which are being initiated and put forward by the Secretary of the Treasury.

Senator MOYNIHAN. Thank you, Mr. Chairman.

The CHAIRMAN. Senator Grassley, and then Senator Baucus.

Senator GRASSLEY. Dr. Greenspan, is inflation or the risk of potential inflation sufficiently in check so that interest rates will not have to be raised in the near future?

Dr. GREENSPAN. Senator, I do not know the answer to that. We have basically put in place a set of policies in which what we endeavor to do is to find that set of policies, that Federal Reserve policy particularly, which will maximize long-term, sustainable economic growth.

As a consequence of that, we are constantly monitoring all elements of emerging inflationary instabilities in which, to be sure, the price inflation—commodity price, product price inflation, consumer price inflation—is by far the most important indicator.

But we also have to look at other elements which indicate instability in the system, as I indicated in my prepared remarks, asset price patterns, as well as the dollar exchange rate, which also indirectly can contribute to inflationary instability. So, we are monitoring a wide variety of factors.

As I am sure you know, the Federal Open Market Committee is meeting early next week and we will be discussing at length what the renewed view of the outlook has been since our last meeting. That is about as much as I can say at this moment, Senator.

Senator GRASSLEY. I assume that means you are going to increase interest rates. [Laughter]

Dr. Greenspan, you probably are one of the most non-political people in town, and I appreciate that, but sometimes you do make statements that do bring about political comment; maybe most of your statements do.

Anyway, with regard to the CPI statement that you made last week and its overestimation, some are making the political argument that Social Security will be effectively cut since COLAs are based on that CPI. I know the Democrats in my State are jumping all over this as a back doorway to cut Social Security. So, I would appreciate your reaction to these sorts of attacks.

Dr. GREENSPAN. Yes. Senator, it is not an endeavor to cut Social Security. The Congress put in place, approximately 20 years ago, an indexing of Social Security and a number of other benefits, as you know. The basic purpose of that was to keep the retirement payment whole in real terms, so that the cost of living was fully adjusted for.

It now appears, in retrospect, that the way we calculate the Consumer Price Index, has effectively over-indexed all of these programs and, in that sense, in real terms, meaning overadjusted for what the true cost of living has been over the years, rather than holding, as the law states, beneficiary payments whole, it has been inadvertently increasing them.

Now, if the Congress meant to do that, then I think the Congress should pass a law and adjust what the basic purpose of the indexing programs was a couple of decades ago. But if, in fact, the purpose was to meet what the law said in my judgment, we should have an adjustment that should take into effect the fact that it is generally well-known, to a greater or lesser extent, that it is biased upward.

It is true that, as far as the beneficiaries of Social Security are concerned, that the mix of the types of prices they pay probably does mean that they pay, on average, maybe 0.2 to 0.3 percentage points more than the average cost of living.

So that if one were to make an adjustment of the type I am discussing, one, you make an adjustment in the total index, and where there are beneficiaries over 62 or 65 where there are indications that there is a higher increase in inflation, largely because of the extra weight of health care, that that adjustment should be made as well.

The net effect, however, would be to significantly reduce the measure of the CPI so that the index that would be employed by the Social Security Administration, for example, would be a more appropriate measure of what the true change in the cost of living is.

Now, I separate this discussion from another issue, which is, what should the Bureau of Labor Statistics be doing to adjust for this bias? They are doing a great deal. I mean, they are fully aware that these biases exist and, indeed, are working assiduously to endeavor to lower the bias.

But, so long as we have a fixed-weight index which serves our purposes for other reasons, that bias will exist, and so long as we do certain types of sampling of prices and rotating of panels in the way we address the pricing relationships among various different products and the way we handle new goods that have just come on the scene, so long as those problems exist, our measured Consumer Price Index will overestimate the true cost of living.

I would suggest that we separate the issue of the professional problems that are associated with the improvement in the CPI from a different issue, which is, how do we appropriately obtain what the underlying cost of living really is in a manner to so index benefit programs and income taxes as to effectively capture the purpose of Congressional intent?

Senator GRASSLEY. Thank you.

The CHAIRMAN. Senator Baucus, and then Senator Chafee.

Senator BAUCUS. Thank you, Mr. Chairman.

Dr. Greenspan, I would like to change the course of this discussion a little bit, if I could, from the abstract to the general, down to the more specific and concrete. The data which you testified to and which is commonly known in the financial press, on average, is not bad, I mean, with the relatively low inflation rate and unemployment rate, and not bad growth rate.

What strikes me though, is those are totals, those are aggregates, and really conceal a lot of economic grief and hardship that a lot of people in this country suffer. Labor Secretary Reich pointed out to many of us just last week that Shaquille O'Neil is, I think, 7′1″, he is 4′8″, and on average they are 5′10″. The average totally just states the reality of the disparities. Everyone knows that income disparities in this country are increasing. The rich are getting richer. That is fine. I do not discourage anyone who works hard to improve his or her income. But there are a lot of people who are not in on this. For example, in my State, I was talking to a home builder. First of all, interest rates are making it very difficult to buy homes in my state. Very difficult. Partly because inflation has pushed home prices up, and, second, the interest rate makes it much more expensive. Ten years ago in Planet Valley, a very popular part of our State, the average three-bedroom home was $56,000; today it is over $106,000–$110,000.

I went to the home builder and asked him, why are people so angry? You pick it up at home. Answer: I pay a journeyman carpenter $14.50 an hour, including overtime, good wages, but when he leaves he cannot afford a home. He has got to go out and live in a trailer someplace and drive a long ways. He cannot live in the kind of homes that he is building.

So I am asking you to just explain to the American people, some of whom maybe watching here. By the people, I mean people whose incomes are between $25,000 and, say, $75,000, two-wage earning families, having a heck of a time making ends meet, who face high interest rates. They hear all this wonderful talk about growth rates, inflation, and all this. It does not mean anything to the person trying to make ends meet, trying to buy a home.

What can you say to the fellow out there, that carpenter, who is working hard, but with high interest rates and high inflation rates and real estate costs, cannot buy a home, or to the average wage earner who also is facing the tremendous economic anxiety that we all know exists?

Dr. GREENSPAN. Senator, the evidence you point out is quite accurate. That is, most all analysts of income distributions have been very acutely aware that since the late 1970's there has been a fairly pronounced increasing dispersion of incomes and, as you put it, the rich get richer and the poor get poorer.

That is not exactly correct, but it is capturing, sort of generally, what has been going on.

The reason, as best we can judge, for this phenomenon is the continued extension, and perhaps acceleration, of technology in our society. It is the inevitable result of progress that an increasing proportion of our gross domestic product is intellectual as distinct from physical. That is, it is ideas which basically create value added.

If we were to, for example, add up all of the physical tons of output in this economy today, it would be only modestly higher than the aggregate amount of, say, iron ore, coal, steel, all of that physical production which we produced almost 100 years ago. Most of the gains are ideas because we find that the same function of a physical thing is now created in small units. I mean, radios used to be big and now they are small, and the like.

Senator BAUCUS. I appreciate that.

Dr. GREENSPAN. What I want to get at here is, what is happening to this whole process is that the technology that is implicit in that has created a situation in which education has become a crucial question in the position in the income scale.

That is, college educated and even high school educated people are finding that their income levels relative to those with lesser educations are continuously rising. It is the value of ideas which are separating our society.

Senator BAUCUS. If I might just quickly follow up on that point. Assuming that it was the goal of the Federal Reserve to focus in on that large group of people, what would the Federal Reserve/monetary policy be?

Dr. GREENSPAN. Yes. I have discussed this, actually, with the Secretary of Labor, my good friend Bob Reich, on many, many occasions. And what we recognize is that macroeconomic policy cannot address this problem; it is an education/training issue.

The reason why he and a number of other economists were studying this phenomenon and are focusing on the question of education and training is that there are no tools that we at the Federal Reserve can use to help this because we can only have one interest rate to affect the whole economy.

We cannot differentiate because of the nature of what a central bank is, nor can overall fiscal policy. Specific program-directed policies to assuage these imbalances are the only way to come at this problem.

So, in that regard, we at the Federal Reserve cannot improve that situation. I wish we could, but we do not have—and, indeed, monetary policy does not have—the capability of doing that.

Senator BAUCUS. You did not fully answer my question, but we will get this later. Thank you.

The CHAIRMAN. Senator Chafee, then Senator Rockefeller.

Senator CHAFEE. Thank you, Mr. Chairman.

Dr. Greenspan, you say on page seven of your testimony, "There can be no doubt that the persistence of a large Federal budget deficit represents in the minds of many individuals a potential risk."

On page 8 you then go on to say, "The Federal deficit drains off a large share of a regrettably small pool of domestic private savings, thus contributing further, perhaps to an even greater degree, to the elevation of real rates of interest in the economy."

The vast majority of analysts would agree that in the United States the current sizable Federal deficits and the projected growth of those deficits over the decades ahead are a significant element in this story, i.e., high, real, long-term rates around the world.

Now, both parties seem to be espousing tax cuts. The President last night talked about a tax cut for the middle class. In the Contract with America in the House they are talking about a $500 tax credit for each child, which would cost $120 billion over 5 years. They are talking of backing off from including 85 percent of Social

88-545 0 - 95 - 2

Security as taxable income and reducing it to 50 percent. That would cost $17 billion over 5 years.

Now, suppose we proceeded in the Congress of the United States in making the spending cuts that we are all talking about—spending cuts, and we did no tax cuts—and used all of that revenue to reduce the deficit, what would you think of that approach; what would that yield us?

Dr. GREENSPAN. Senator, I would say that the major up-front priority for our fiscal system is to get spending down or, even more appropriately, as I think is correct, the rate of growth significantly slowed. That is the number one priority in looking for fiscal stability.

I must admit, I am a little chagrined that the Kerrey-Danforth Commission on Entitlements was not taken with a greater degree of seriousness than I believe it was. We not only have got a spending problem which extends through the year 2002, we have got a spending problem which really accelerates as we get into the 21st century.

Unless we come to grips with that, it is going to be very difficult to bring these real, long-term interest rate premiums down because 30-year bonds pick up the expected degree of inflation or instability which affects real rates through the maturity of the bond instrument so that a 30-year bond that we sell now goes through the first quarter of the 21st century.

If we do not get spending down and get it on a trajectory which is far more related to the growth in the underlying tax base of this economy, we are going to have chronic fiscal problems.

Senator CHAFEE. I would like to just interrupt, if I might, there. Everybody seems to agree that we should reduce the spending. I mean, there is bold talk of major steps. But then they follow up with proposals to use some of this money for tax cuts. But, if you have tax cuts commensurate with the reduction in spending, you have not reduced your deficit a nickel.

Dr. GREENSPAN. Absolutely.

Senator CHAFEE. My question specifically is, would we not make the country a lot better off, reduce interest rates, improve the prosperity and employment, if we went ahead with the spending cuts or the tax cuts?

Dr. GREENSPAN. Senator, it depends very crucially on the question of how much spending cuts are involved. I mean, I can do the arithmetic and calculate that if there are enough spending cuts you can both reach a balanced budget, or, as far as I am concerned, it would not be a disaster if we ended up with a surplus because that would help the saving problem. But, if we cut spending enough, there is room for cutting taxes.

Senator CHAFEE. But nobody is suggesting that that is going to get us to a zero deficit.

Dr. GREENSPAN. That is what I am getting at. Sure.

The point at issue is, first of all, I must say that I, like most economists, think, if you are going to cut taxes, do it at the marginal tax rate and the type of general tax reduction which does not affect marginal rates does not strike me as one that affects the efficiency of the economy very much.

But, if you are asking me, do I think that deficit reduction is the first priority and tax cuts are second to that, the answer is, yes. I would like to see both happen.

But, if we cannot do both, we have to at least get started on very significant reductions in the budget deficit.

Senator CHAFEE. Thank you.

The CHAIRMAN. Senator Rockefeller, then Senator Conrad.

Senator ROCKEFELLER. Thank you, Mr. Chairman.

Dr. Greenspan, one of the problems around here, it seems to me, is that if somebody says they are for tax cuts and they are for fairly large tax cuts, people assume automatically that they want to somehow appease the rich or make the rich richer, or that they have a philosophy which we, on our side, would say would be Republican.

On the other hand, if somebody talks about investing in infrastructure, it has almost become a code word for spending money and, therefore, sort of irresponsible economic activity.

So, my question is the following. It seems to me that when Republicans talk about—this is not political, I am just trying to say this—cutting taxes and cutting spending, that they make the assumption that the private market will make allocation of the results of that in such a way as to cause the economy and the American people, in the first instance, to grow, and in the second instance, to become more productive through education, which you just talked about, and infrastructure. You can see what is happening in Kobe, Japan without infrastructure, just everything stops in the way of economic activity. Is there not a real trade off here in a serious discussion as between the short-term interests of our economy?

Now, business, as we all know, is under tremendous quarterly pressure to produce profits. That has been the case, and continues to be the case. We talk about longer view, but ultimately the marketplace demands results—and even Japan now is beginning to switch in that direction—so that the short-term interest of cutting taxes and cutting spending, but for the longer term interest there has to be the infrastructure, there has to be the education, there has to be getting kids ready for technology, there has to be lifelong learning. I am told that Hansford out in Washington is $100–$200 billion in clean-up of toxic waste. That is something, like the S&L, something that we do not want to do, but we have to do; that does not continue productivity of anybody, but just concentrating on productivity, on making people and the economy more responsive to the global economy. Does there not have to be an intelligent balance as between the short-term and the long-term interests reflected in public policy?

Dr. GREENSPAN. Senator, I think you are putting your finger on what is a major issue of debate among economists. The real crucial question is, what is the economic return on infrastructure? And there is a large dispute that has been going on in recent years about to what extent does the productivity of our economy depend on public infrastructure?

I think I am safe in saying that there were very loud voices on both sides of that question, and I am also safe in saying that the conclusion is not universal. The reason is that it is a particularly difficult statistical issue.

I mean, we can assert that education is of value, and certainly it is, and one would basically assume that increased school buildings and increased school infrastructure would help, and we go through this whole series of evaluations. The trouble is, it is not all that easy to differentiate between various different types of infrastructure to make determinations of which are most productive and which are not. I am not, today, going to get involved in trying to suggest where the answers are because I do not follow the research as closely as I would like to.

My only important point which I think is relevant to the longer term is the deficit, per se, is a very negative problem that this country confronts. And before we get——

Senator ROCKEFELLER. But Dr. Greenspan, you have just made my premise because, as I was talking about infrastructure—which does not mean just physical but the productivity of people—you then, it seems to me—maybe I falsely characterize it—then assume that I was not interested in lowering the deficit. I am. I am saying that, in the lowering of the deficit.

I mean, on this side we are all now on board on that. In the lowering of the deficit, the difference between how you lower it so as to allow room for foreign subsidies—which Kent Conrad would disagree with me on—as opposed to education and the critical technologies. No American fighter plane can take off without Japanese computer chips, et cetera, and this type of thing.

Dr. GREENSPAN. Well, you know, it is an interesting issue because these are value judgments, in part. To a very large extent, you cannot analytically draw the types of distinctions—in some cases you probably can, but in most cases it is very difficult—to judge the marginal difference between what tax cuts do and what expenditure increases do, for example.

It depends on where one looks at the relative tradeoffs. I tend to be one of those looking over the structure of the various trade-offs, and, as best I can judge, the way the society functions is that the smaller the government the better, and I come out with, therefore, a tendency to be more in favor of cutting taxes wherever we can and reducing expenditures.

But I recognize that these are value judgments, and that it really gets to a fundamental view of one's conception of the way the society ought to function. I think, to a limited extent we can analytically solve the problem and make it a scientific issue, but I think we would be surprised at how little our scientific tools can address the types of question that you are raising, Senator?.

Senator ROCKEFELLER. Thank you, Mr. Chairman.

The CHAIRMAN. Senator Conrad, then Senator Murkowski.

Senator CONRAD. Thank you, Mr. Chairman. I would like to go back to Mexico for a minute because we hear a lot of talk in Washington about letting the markets work. We hear that very frequently. I think most people believe that is a policy that makes sense, letting the markets work.

In this case, investors made a bet. They wanted high return and so they invested in Mexico and they took a high risk to justify that high return. Now, things are bad. And what do we do, are we letting the markets work? Oh, no. In this case we are rushing in and telling the taxpayers they are to cover the bets of the folks who put their money in Mexico to get a high return.

I find it very hard to justify to the taxpayers back home why they should put their dollars at risk to bail out folks on Wall Street, folks in Tokyo, folks in Bonn, who bet in order to get a high rate of return. What is the answer to those people who are asked to put their money at risk to bail out those who made a bad bet?

Dr. GREENSPAN. I think that is a very good question, Senator. As I indicated in my testimony before the House Banking Committee earlier this morning, the negative side of loan guarantees is it creates what economists call a disincentive structure, a so-called moral hazard, to the way markets work. To that extent, as I indicated earlier, we need a very structured conditionality to make certain that we do not distort the markets more than we would otherwise do.

Senator CONRAD. But do you not distort the market immediately? The markets have sent us a very clear signal. The Mexicans kept that peso pegged at a high level for their own internal political reasons.

Now, the markets have said, hey, it does not make sense, this does not add up. We are walking in and saying, well, we are going to repeal the laws of the market; we are going to cover this for you. We are saying to our taxpayers, you cover the bad bet that these investors made. How do we justify that?

Dr. GREENSPAN. Well, let me get to that point, Senator. First of all, the individual investors who have lost in this situation are not going to recoup with loan guarantees because it is very difficult to see that the type of loan guaranty that is being discussed will change the markets very much, that the losses that have been made or incurred are going to be reversed.

What you may well say is that further losses would be prevented by a loan guaranty, and that is true, and that is the purpose. The purpose is not to bail anybody out. They have already lost a big chunk of cash and they are not going to get any of that back, except if things improve dramatically.

So, we are not recommending that people get bailed out, what we are recommending is that we basically attain a situation which is stabilized because we are concerned that the contagion effect of the Mexican problems will have broader implications to the United States than we would like.

This is not an issue of trying to bail out markets. The effort, basically, is an endeavor to stabilize them. If you are asking me, do I think that it is a good idea to go in and intervene in markets, I will argue very strenuously, it is only in very extraordinary circumstances. And, as I indicated earlier this morning, I think that the loan guaranty is the least worst of the alternatives that confront us.

If we did not have the serious potential unraveling problems associated with this, I would not be supportive of it. Does it have secondary negative consequences because it distorts markets? Yes, it does. Is that good? The answer is, no, it is not good. Do we have a better alternative to stabilize the system? My answer is, I do not know of any.

Senator CONRAD. Let me just say that it sounds very much like, let markets work unless the big boys get in trouble, and then we march in and the taxpayers pick up the tag.

It is kind of an eerie reminder of the S&L fiasco, it is kind of an eerie reminder of almost every one of these situations where you have "too big to fail." All of a sudden, if the big boys put their money on the line in order to get a high return and they make a bad bet and they go out and take high risks, then all the rest of us come in and pick up the bill.

You know, it is a great system. I would like to have that kind of investment principle in my portfolio; I go out there and take a high risk to get a high return and I get it, but, if things go bad, somebody else comes in and covers my bad bet.

Dr. GREENSPAN. But the bet is not being covered. That loss is there, it is going to stay there. Indeed——

Senator CONRAD. Well, are you telling me that this is not going to lead to some market recovery in Mexico?

Dr. GREENSPAN. At the moment I think what we are looking for is market stabilization. If the markets recover because they stabilize faster, then I would say there are fortunate people out there. But that is not our purpose.

Let me just say, further, Senator, a substantial part of these big investors are mutual funds and mutual funds, as you know, are made up with tens of thousands of smaller investors.

So, I do not deny that there may be some big guys in there, which you allude to, and I do not deny there may be a couple which, as a result of this loan guaranty, get more than they deserve. I will not deny that. I think it is good I do not. But the alternative of not doing something to stabilize the situation, in my judgment, is a major mistake.

The CHAIRMAN. I might add, on the S&Ls, that is exactly the same kind of people we were bailing out. It was not the big boys, it was the Aunt Minnies who had their $35,000 of life's savings in the S&L and it was gone, and we had promised that we would protect her.

Senator CONRAD. Well, Mr. Chairman, I just have to say in this case I think the big boys are on Wall Street, the big boys are in Tokyo, the big boys are in Bonn. They made a bet. They went down there to get a high return, they took a high risk, and things went bad, and now all the rest of us ride to the rescue. I tell you, it does not apply to most folks in life. That is not the way letting markets work functions. In this case, that is what is occurring.

The CHAIRMAN. We will go to Senator Murkowski, then Senator Bradley.

Senator MURKOWSKI. Thank you, Mr. Chairman.

Dr. Greenspan, good morning. I think in your opening remarks you were optimistic about the advance of the economy, inflation, jobs, growth, and so forth, but there are a couple of areas you did not discuss but were later brought up.

Of course, one of them is the deficit, on which I would like to elaborate a little bit more. But I would also like to call your attention to the trade deficit which is at an all-time high, at, I think, $154 billion. We cannot seem to get a handle on it. Half of it is roughly the cost of imported oil, and we are importing over 50 percent now, with no relief in sight. We have a few domestic alternatives but we cannot seem to jar them loose from the environmental community. The other half is our trade with Japan. It is a very difficult time now to address that with Japan because of the disaster in Kobe.

But, as we look at the CBO figures of January 5th, we see current relief relative to the deficit, but then it begins to go up in the year 1997 to $207 billion, $224 billion, $222 billion, $253 billion, on and on. And, of course, the interest cost goes up. The interest cost moves to $260 billion, to $270 billion, to $279 billion, and so forth.

I have done some quick calculations, and if we did not have this interest cost we would have a surplus by the end of year 2005 of about $341 billion, which could, of course, reduce the accumulated debt.

You and I remember, back in 1980 I was in the private sector lending, making commercial loans, and the interest rate was 20.5 percent. That is a terrible set of realities to reflect upon, but we have a reality here of the potential of interest rates going up, and what that would mean to the deficit. We are looking at increased debt accumulated overall—what is it, $4.8 trillion, or thereabouts—we are looking at increased interest costs.

And, as we look at Mexico today, we are faced with the reality that here is a country that borrowed too much, and we have got a problem now relative to whether or not the Congress should provide the authority for loan guarantees. Now, we have seen the statement by Bill Seidman. He says it is a market judgment, a mistake. Mexico was overdoing a good thing, they borrowed too much money; why should anyone bail them out?

Others have said, and you said in your testimony today, that this was a situation that was known about for some time. Last summer, Mexico's foreign debt had become dangerously high. We are moving now as a consequence of the crisis as opposed to mandating reforms that could have been, perhaps, structured in the Mexican economy but were not, for political reasons and other things. So, we are seeing this evolution of more debt and now we are faced with the question of what kind of guarantees we are going to have.

I would like to know, as a matter of factual reference, just how much collateralization we can expect. I know when the new Secretary of Treasury came to see me he was talking about fully collateralizing the guarantees associated with the Mexican funding.

I am not sure, and I have yet to get a straight answer from the administration, just how much collateral is really available relative to the oil that is unattached. I wonder if you could enlighten us in this regard, what can we really expect as far as collateralization?

Again, you and I are going to be seeing a lot of each other about debt because I am also concerned about the Canadian debt and the precedent that we are potentially setting in this regard with the collateralization of the Mexican debt. Just how much collateral is out there? Is it risk-free to the U.S. taxpayer in the sense that it is fully collateralized?

Dr. GREENSPAN. Senator, let me just say that the loan guarantee program that the Treasury and the administration is putting together does not increase Mexico's debt, it merely is an endeavor, largely, to shift short-term debt to longer-term debt.

Senator MURKOWSKI. I understand.

Dr. GREENSPAN. So the aggregate debt and their debt service charges should not be significantly altered.

Senator MURKOWSKI. No. But that is what got them there.

Dr. GREENSPAN. Absolutely. There is no question about that. On the issue of the backing for the guarantees should they be initiated, the current discussion is to have oil proceeds automatically, instead of being moved from the purchaser of Mexican oil directly to Mexico City, go to the Federal Reserve Bank of New York, essentially an offset to backing particular guarantees.

The Mexicans export approximately $6–$7 billion American dollars in crude oil and products. The technical ability in order to get all of that is clearly there. My own judgment is, if we took too much of the collateral it would make it difficult for Mexico, but there is, nonetheless, a very substantial amount of potential oil revenues which are not legally collateral. It is a different type of assured payment, but it is there.

The question is, to what level do we expect the loan program to go so that these guarantees would be activated? As best we can judge, it should be a relatively modest amount.

And if it is a modest amount—because only a modest amount is really required to solve the problem—you want a much larger facility basically to enable the markets to feel comfortable with that—the amount of facility that will be employed is relatively small. So, as a consequence of that, the amount of actual oil proceeds that would be involved could be relatively modest.

An important issue not to forget, however, is that a crucial part of this is a very substantial, up-front payment by the Mexicans for purposes of endeavoring to pay for the presumed risk that is involved in these guarantees, so that the probability of American taxpayer loss is reasonably well containable.

There are scenarios which you can create in which there would be losses, but I would say that the probabilities of that happening are quite low and I would suspect that we have access to very significant oil proceeds.

I think it is really up to the United States to determine just how much of that we would wish to take on, and that really becomes a function of how far the guarantees would have to go before the system stabilized.

Senator MURKOWSKI. Well, Mr. Chairman, I do not want to prolong this, other than it would be very beneficial for this Senator to have some idea of what the loan agreement on the guarantees covers because when you extend an agreement to $30–$40 billion, you potentially are going to have the exposure of being called for that amount and you have to be able to exercise unattached collateral as necessary to cover whatever the exposure might be.

I am still not satisfied that we are getting a qualified answer relative to just how much risk is associated with that, and that may be how much we are going to be called upon to guarantee at any given time. I understand that, but I am still interested in the availability of collateral and the ability to assign that collateral.

The CHAIRMAN. Senator Bradley, and then Senator Graham.

Senator MURKOWSKI. Thank you, Mr. Chairman.

Senator BRADLEY. Thank you very much, Mr. Chairman.

Dr. Greenspan, you alluded to the change in the international financial system and portfolio investment flowing across national boundaries. How much portfolio investment flows across national boundaries, would you say, on a daily basis?

Dr. GREENSPAN. The number is larger than any number we can name, I suspect.

Senator BRADLEY. So it is in the trillions of dollars.

Dr. GREENSPAN. Oh, yes. But, it is hard to know. We do not measure it all. All we know is, we can pick up some of the extent of the size through what the so-called Fed-wire is in the United States and CHIPS.

Senator BRADLEY. So just to mention it, it is a very, very big number.

Dr. GREENSPAN. Yes.

Senator BRADLEY. Now, I think that the whole loan guaranty is going to, in some ways, hinge on your ability and the administration's ability to articulate this, so this is an opportunity for you. Tell me. You said, "Gee, if this does not happen, bad things happen out there." Now, we know there may be increased immigration, and we know a drop in U.S. exports.

But what is your larger fear about the international financial system and how does that play out for, say the worker in Perth-Amboy, NJ, or somebody who works in a factory in Pennsylvania?

Dr. GREENSPAN. First of all, let me just say that the worker in Perth-Amboy, NJ, which I have visited many, many times in my life, is, to a very large extent, buttressed by the extraordinary efficacy of the international financial system. That worker does not know that; indeed, nobody realizes where one's standard of living comes from.

But it is readily apparent to economists who try to understand where the standard of living of the United States generally comes from. There is no question that international trade is a very important factor in our standard of living, and the facilitation of trade is our international financial system.

So, what we have got to be certain of as we oversee the total structure of what makes the world work, is that we make certain that we do not put that system at risk. That is crucial for the steelworker in Bethlehem, PA, or a retail service person in Texas.

Senator BRADLEY. How is it at risk? Specifically tell us, how is it at risk?

Dr. GREENSPAN. Well, first of all, I do not want to suggest that the whole thing unravels. I am just saying, if Mexico defaults on its obligations, it will create the types of problems which we should not expose ourselves to.

Senator BRADLEY. What types of problems?

Dr. GREENSPAN. Well, the one thing we can do if there are, say, Chapter 11s, or as far as municipalities are concerned in the United States, Chapter 9s, we can have an organized type of liquidation of debts which are not payable. That is very difficult to handle with a sovereign government.

And what would concern me is that should we find ourselves in default, that is, the Mexicans are in default of substantial issues——

Senator BRADLEY. So they are in default to all these mutual funds?

Dr. GREENSPAN. They are in default for a lot of different things.

Senator BRADLEY. So, what happens?

Dr. GREENSPAN. I do not know what happens, very specifically. I can guess, I can make presumptions.

Senator BRADLEY. But you are a contingency planner.

Dr. GREENSPAN. Yes. I am a contingency planner sometimes.

Senator BRADLEY. So what are the contingencies you are planning for; what is your fear out there?

Dr. GREENSPAN. There are a lot of contingencies I plan for, a lot of them with very low probabilities.

And what concerns me is, if I gave you a low probability contingency it will come out that I am somehow forecasting some terrible event is going to happen. I am not going to say that because I do not think it is going to happen.

But I do think it is important for us to be sufficiently up front so that we fend off even the low probability events from happening before they take on a degree of destabilizing character which I do not think is the type of thing we ought to risk.

Senator BRADLEY. Look. What difference does it make whether capital flows into Mexico, or flows into Thailand, or flows into the Philippines from abroad; what difference does it make to anybody?

Dr. GREENSPAN. It should.

Senator BRADLEY. Why?

Dr. GREENSPAN. Because basically if we argue that the level of international trade has a significant effect on our standards of living, anything which would materially prevent that from happening—and international financial disruptions would—is to our advantage to prevent from occurring if we can.

Senator BRADLEY. So that basically what we are trying to do is keep the current international financial system together, and there is now, basically, capital flight in Mexico, flowing out of there, also capital flight out of a number of other third-world countries that have attracted capital in the last several years.

Dr. GREENSPAN. Yes.

Senator BRADLEY. And that is what we want to prevent.

Dr. GREENSPAN. If we can.

Senator BRADLEY. Now, U.S. interest rates play a role here.

Dr. GREENSPAN. Yes.

Senator BRADLEY. If you raised U.S. interest rates, the giant sucking sound is going to be money coming out of Mexico into the United States, so all of the people around here have been urging you not to raise interest rates.

There is another reason not to raise interest rates. There is the very real probability that, if you raise those interest rates, the sucking sound of capital out of Mexico endangers the $40 billion loan guaranty that you are here today testifying in favor of. Would you not agree?

Dr. GREENSPAN. I would say that the basic function of Federal Reserve policy is focused on long-term, sustainable growth in the

United States. To the extent that we successfully are able to implement that, that will help Mexico, will help all of our trading partners, and will help the international financial system.

Senator BRADLEY. You just said today that you have interest rates, you have inflation, and then you have to have an interest rate margin to attract capital from abroad.

Dr. GREENSPAN. Well, let me reverse the question,

Senator If it is good not to raise them, it must be better to lower them. And if we were to lower them, let us assume, and we created instability in the United States, the presumption would be that capital would flow back to Mexico because of that and create a much improved environment. I will tell you, I do not believe that.

The CHAIRMAN. Senator Graham, then Senator D'Amato.

Senator GRAHAM. Mr. Chairman, I had not intended to ask a question on Mexico, but I cannot restrain myself. The International Monetary Fund was established, in part, to provide an international agency that could deal with these kinds of financial crises. Could you evaluate how well it has functioned in the situation of Mexico and what that says about how well it is likely to function in the future and any reforms that would be called for?

Dr. GREENSPAN. Senator, I do not know enough about first-hand relationships and so called Article IV relationships between the IMF and the Mexican Government.

What I can say is, the size of the IMF is relatively small as, indeed, are the other international financial institutions when one compares it to the types of issues of private institutions in which capital flows back and forth across national boundaries.

The International Monetary Fund—which was, as you will recall, set up in 1944 as a result of the Bretton Woods agreement—has the central purpose to try to stabilize capital flows in an environment in which there were fixed exchange rates and very modest capital flows.

The environment we face today is really quite dramatically different. The size of the flows are horrendous.

My impression is that, while the IMF presumably has the capability of being of considerable assistance in a situation such as Mexico, it is by no means clear to me that they themselves, with their current balance sheet and current authorities, can fully address the type of problem that we at the Federal Reserve and our colleagues at the Treasury have unearthed.

Senator GRAHAM. Dr. Greenspan, the question that I had intended to ask is sparked by the sentence in your statement that says, "For the Congress, a crucial focus should be, one, continuing the process of fiscal consolidation and, two, rectifying the secular shortfall in domestic savings that is limiting the growth of our Nation's productive potential."

Would you give two or three priorities under each of those two areas that you say should be the crucial focus for Congress? What should we be doing in order to continue the process of fiscal consolidation and rectifying secular shortfalls and domestic savings?

Dr. GREENSPAN. I would say, if I were to just list a few things which I think would be helpful for the Congress to consider is, this is, as I indicated before, Senator, the results of the Entitlement Commission which indicated there were some very serious problems in some of our social insurance programs as we get into the 21st century.

In my judgment, there is very little controversy on the fact that those problems exist or on their order of magnitude which suggests to me that the Congress can make adjustments in those programs today, effective, say, in the year 2005 or 2015, and have a very material effect on the long-term fiscal outlook of this country.

And I suspect that were we to do that in a credible manner, that the inflation premiums embodied in long-term interest rates, which I have mentioned earlier, would come down today.

What our political experience has been is that it is very difficult to approach entitlement programs when the problems are right on top of us, but I suspect they are far easier to resolve with a very long lead time.

And I am not at all certain that events are going to significantly change between now and the turn of the century. If not, it is far better to address those longer-term problems now and get them out of the way when I think they are far easier to come to grips with.

Senator GRAHAM. And what about the second issue, rectifying secular shortfalls and domestic savings rates?

Dr. GREENSPAN. Senator, strangely, it is the same answer because, while we have got innumerable programs which are endeavoring to create saving incentives, recent history suggests that none of them work all that well and that, if we would remove the Federal budget deficit or significantly reduce it because it acts as a net claim against private domestic saving, we would improve national saving, and, presumably, improve our capability to maintain a higher level of capital investment and, hence, productivity and economic growth.

Senator GRAHAM. Thank you.

The CHAIRMAN. Senator D'Amato, then Senator Moseley-Brown.

Senator D'AMATO. Thank you, Mr. Chairman.

Dr. Greenspan, good to see you.

Dr. GREENSPAN. Thank you.

Senator D'AMATO. Let me first say, when we initially spoke about the loan guaranty program, I suggested that if we were going to do it, it was analogous to building a bulkhead. I grew up on the water. I have seen people invest in a bulkhead—with pilings driven 12 feet down, that did little, if anything, because of two or three good storms—who spent a lot of money and that bulkhead was washed out, as opposed to spending a little more or putting up some more capital investing and putting in the bulkhead and driving it down 35 or 40 feet and ensuring for the next 40 years that you were not going to have that problem with the attendant loss in erosion.

So I support doing this, but we have to do it the right way. You do not do it part of the way, you do not come in with something less and try to do it cheap, $20–$25 billion. That does not make sense.

Having said that, as I have gotten into this whole area and met with the administration and their people over a period of time, I can say to you, they have not been as forthcoming with the information that about a half a dozen of my colleagues, both Republicans and Democrats, have requested. For example, when do these notes come due? Who are the holders of these notes to the best that we can identify? And I understand that we may not have that information.

Dr. GREENSPAN. Are we talking about the tesobonos?

Senator D'AMATO. Yes, the tesobonos. How much of it is held by American interest that we can ascertain? How much of it is held by Japanese or other interests? What plans, if any, do we have in terms of burden sharing?

The possibility of restructuring the guarantee so that it does not flow within an 18-month period of time because at the end of that 18 months we lose leverage; the possibility of shrinking the repayment schedule so that we reduce the risk from 10 years to somewhat less.

These are suggestions I put forth in a manner in which I wish to see if there is something we can do. We have asked some 19 question that we submitted. It has been more than a week now and we have not had a response.

What we have is the administration sending out various Secretaries and other people attempting to buttonhole one Senator after the other, telling them of the doom and gloom, telling them if we do not go along with this that there are going to be incredible immigration problems, et cetera.

I suggest to you that that is superficial at this point in time. We understand the importance of this relationship. We understand the trade, the commerce. We understand that if you have a collapse in Mexico there will be fallouts.

Having said that, you talked about structured conditionality. I have to suggest to you that, as I get into this more and more, it seems to me that that will be difficult, if not impossible, and that we have to look to the stability of the Mexican Government.

We have been given to believe that it was much more stable than appears to be the case. I do not know if we can get that conditionality. Let me give you one other. In terms of putting up the resources of oil as collateral, it would appear that that is going to pose a great problem. I wonder if we kid ourselves and have an agreement that is not worth too much because the person who signs that agreement is unable to enforce it because his own party is in disarray, and because there is literally boiling underneath the aspects of what one might call a revolution.

I will give you my thought on this, because I do not mean to be telling you one thing and going in another direction. It seems that, given the lack of stability, even if you drive that bulkhead down 40 feet, I think you may have to look at the stability of the situation and one would have to question the wisdom in dealing with the situation that we have now. I also have to say that Senator Conrad posed some very interesting points about investment and risk.

When you invest, as they did in tesobonos, and got 25 percent returns, people are saying that is a pretty risky speculative investment. Should we at some point be coming in to take them off that? I do not know. I do not think so. It is far different from an S&L where there was an implied guarantee by the American Government that, if we were going to be in a position where savers lost their money, we would hold them harmless. We never made that guarantee.

Last, and not least, I asked myself this question, and I see my time is almost up. Why is it that we do not ask the Mexican Government—and I think we have to work with the government—to restructure the debt?

Why should somebody be able to come and say, here is a tesobono with $1 million carrying a 20 percent return; we are now going to pay you $1,200,000. No. We are sorry. You bought this.

We are not in a position to pay, but we will restructure it and we will use as collateral our oil—we will, the Mexicans—and by the way, we will pay you back over 5 years, and by the way, we will not pay you back dollar for dollar, and by the way, we will not pay you 20 percent, but maybe we will give you 60 cents on the dollar, or 50 cents, or 70 cents.

I mean, it is done every day. If we are over here attempting to imply or impose conditions, it is not going to work. We do not have the power to impose those conditions.

So, Mr. Chairman, I want you to know that I have been looking at this carefully. I have not come down on the side of being unalterably opposed. But I tell you, there are many, many obstacles that have to be dealt with before at least this Senator will be willing to go forward and vote for this.

Dr. GREENSPAN. Senator, let me just address that.

The CHAIRMAN. I am not sure that was a question, Alan.

Dr. GREENSPAN. He did ask me a question.

The CHAIRMAN. All right.

Dr. GREENSPAN. It was in the very beginning, and he asked about the data on these tesobonos. I think now there are around 28 billion out there, of which 16 are held by the U.S., and maybe a couple of billion held by other foreigners. The rest are domestic, as best we can make a judgment on it.

Senator D'AMATO. I appreciate that.

But I wanted to be fair, Mr. Chairman, with Dr. Greenspan, because we have attempted to work together. And I have to say he has been the one refreshing light in this whole thing in terms of making himself available and sharing with our committee the information. I wanted to be fair with him and let him know where we are.

Dr. GREENSPAN. Thank you.

The CHAIRMAN. He has been a beacon of light on all matters for 10 years.

Senator Moseley-Braun, and then Senator Pressler.

Senator MOSELEY-BRAUN. Thank you very much, Mr. Chairman. Nice to see you again, Dr. Greenspan.

Dr. GREENSPAN. Thank you.

Senator MOSELEY-BRAUN. We have been talking about a subject that arises as a result of the immense flow of capital into Mexico. I would like, for a moment, to connect the dots between Mexico and Galesburg, IL, Decatur, IL, East St. Louis, IL, Chicago, IL, communities that have suffered from the lack of available capital for investment and development, communities in which there is sometimes unemployment, particularly among young people, as high as 50, 60, 70 percent in some instances.

While, on the one hand, we can talk about the internationalization of these capital flows and that is a good thing, and the like, the fundamental fact is that when you get high yields, 25 percent of those are associated with some risk.

And it appears that the individuals who made the judgments and made the decisions to invest money there either ignored or underestimated what those risks might be and they are now looking to us in Congress to help.

When we are faced, on the one hand, with communities here at home that capital flows miss altogether, there is no money for investment, no money for job creation, giving rise to unemployment and the like, and in situations in communities in which the investments might be less risky than the exotic, trendy even, foreign investments, the yield may not be as high, but certainly the investments would be even sounder.

My question to you would be, why have we not done more to encourage investors who may be affected in this situation to look homeward, if you will, to diversify into America in rural and urban American areas where that investment might be needed and might be productive?

And why is there a willingness to take the risk to meet the demand for capital in Mexico and other emerging markets and not a similar willingness to meet the demand for capital, even at high rates, in many United States communities that need economic development?

Dr. GREENSPAN. Well, Senator, this loan guarantee, assuming that it passes, is not putting new capital into Mexico.

Senator MOSELEY-BRAUN. No.

Dr. GREENSPAN. All it is doing is basically supporting a shift from short-term liabilities to long-term liabilities. It is not a capital inflow in that regard.

Senator MOSELEY-BRAUN. But it is propping up capital that has happened already.

Dr. GREENSPAN. Oh, sure. There is no question of that.

Senator MOSELEY-BRAUN. Yes.

Dr. GREENSPAN. And the issue here from the point of the view of the interest of the United States really relates to the question of where we see potential systemic risks occurring.

The unfortunate difficulty that confronts us is that there are many times when large institutions in this country, for example, fail or are on the edge of failure, and we have this doctrine—which I think is unfortunate, in some respects, but I do not know how we get around it—which is called "Too Big to Fail." That is, there has always been the question that if a very large institution was in serious financial difficulties, that the central bank should bail it out.

Now, the truth of the matter is, I can conceive of situations in which large financial institutions are in financial difficulty and we would not see that their liquidation would be a big problem for everybody else, but there are other occasions.

With an analogy I used a week or so ago, the problem that we have in Mexico is almost as though there is somebody smoking in bed in the building right next door to us and the building is on fire, and if we do not help to put the fire out, our building gets in trouble. And one can argue, well, this is unfair. Indeed, it is unfair. But there are certain things that we have to do to preserve the overall system.

In many respects, this Mexican situation has that characteristic. I do not think that if we had no systemic problems, meaning flow over from Mexico to the United States and elsewhere, that it would be appropriate for us to be doing anything.

Senator MOSELEY-BRAUN. Well, if anything, you have used a wonderful analogy. It seems to me that if, by suggesting that we are willing to come in and put this floor or these guarantees in place, we are only encouraging our neighbors next door and down the street to smoke in bed, particularly at a time when we have done little, if anything, to get rid of the barriers to people even bringing cigarettes into our own house. I mean, that, it seems to me, is the connection and the problem here, or one of the problems. There are a lot of problems that have been raised by members of the committee today.

But, when we have a situation in which there are whole areas of our own country that are not receiving the kind of capital flows, in large part, because people perceive risk associated with investing in these areas. It is not happening at all over there.

But then in the house next door we are saying, all right, if you smoke in bed and the threat is big enough to the block, we are going to do what we can to make sure that there is a fire department standing by.

Dr. GREENSPAN. Well, Senator, that is the reason why Congress has to make choices on various different priorities. In fact, in my testimony this morning before the House Banking Committee I basically said this issue has risen to a point where decisions on this type of activity should not be delegated to unelected officials like myself or my colleagues at the Federal Reserve or at the Treasury, it is an important major political decision for our political leaders.

And one of the reasons we brought this issue to the President and the Congress is because this is the type of choice trade-off which is very difficult to make. We can give our recommendations, but the ultimate choice has got to be the Congress and the President.

The CHAIRMAN. Senator Pressler.

Senator PRESSLER. Thank you very much, Mr. Chairman.

I had some questions on Mexico, but I think you have covered that subject. Let me ask you about inflation once more, to follow up on Senator Grassley's question.

What conditions in the next 5 years could cause a big round of inflation? And is it not true that we need 2–3 percent inflation a year; that that is probably considered a healthy thing; or what level of inflation do you consider healthy?

As you look over the next 5 years, what would be your view of inflation? I know you have raised interest rates to try to prevent inflation. There must be a lot of pressures for inflation. Will those eventually burst forth and we will see a year or two of high inflation?

Dr. GREENSPAN. I would suspect not. I hope not. I presume and hope that the policies of the central bank here have been, to date, adequate to contain such concern. The issue of what the appropriate rate of inflation is, in my judgment, is zero; that is, price stability, in the context I was discussing before, not the CPI being zero because I think CPI is biased upward, but something close to a level of prices which, as I like to put it, business and consumers do not take future price expectations into consideration when they make long-term decisions.

There are arguments that some economists make that it would be desirable to have some level of inflation above zero, largely because it creates greater wage flexibility, in their judgment. I do not agree with that, personally. I do not think the evidence supports it.

We used to have a view back in the 1960's that you needed a little inflation to grease the wheels of the economy and that was a pretty generally held argument.

I do not know anyone who holds that argument in the same sense that they did back then, and we would be far better off to view price stability as the ideal state which maximizes a long-term, sustainable economic growth. I do not think the evidence at this stage is definitive on that question. My guess is, in 5–10 years we will probably look back and say it is definitive.

Senator PRESSLER. All right. Let me ask you a phenomenon that I see. In your testimony you paint, quite accurately I think, a rosy picture of the overall economic indicators of the economic health in our country. But, in fact, you talk to a lot of people on the street and they think we are in trouble.

Is this because businesses are doing well and employees are not? Now, our country seems to be prospering almost in spite of the government because, really, Congress has not done anything to reduce the deficit.

I mean, we have had a lot of activities around here and discussions, but I do not think the White House has done anything either. We have had a lot of rhetoric. It seems that the country is booming in spite of the government, or at least anything we have done down here, we certainly cannot take credit for it.

First of all, is the economy really doing as well as you say it is? I mean, why is there this dichotomy? When I talk to people they say, "God, we are on the verge of a depression or something."

Number two, are all the good things happening in spite of the government?

Dr. GREENSPAN. The economy is, in an average sense——

Senator PRESSLER. In a what?

Dr. GREENSPAN [continuing]. Doing very well, certainly considering our most recent past. Underneath the averages there are problems. My colloquy with Senator Baucus discussing the income distribution problem is clearly one of them.

There are still geographic problems in this country where some areas of the country are doing less well than others, although I must say that in recent months there has apparently been some convergence of activity so that virtually all areas of the economy are doing modestly well to exceptionally well. Even Southern California, which has been for awhile the weakest part of our American economy, is showing signs of picking up.

But, even under the best of circumstances, the best macroeconomic situation you can define, there will always be problems. There will always be some level of unemployment, there will always be people who cannot get jobs who do not have the educational skills that are needed, but the evaluation of the economy is always in an aggregate sense.

The second issue you raise, Senator, which is, how important is the government here is a fascinating issue and what seems to be emerging around the country is that the government is less and less responsible for what goes on in local areas and productiveness in markets.

And I think there is a growing consensus that to allow markets to work and allow individuals freedom from regulations and various different types of enterprise-constraining activities is very beneficial to economic growth.

Senator PRESSLER. Yes.

Dr. GREENSPAN. So, I personally am of the view that government does a lot more than I think it effectively should do.

Senator PRESSLER. And this would be especially true in the small business sector. The less we do in the small business area, the better off they will be.

Dr. GREENSPAN. That is probably an accurate statement, Senator.

The CHAIRMAN. Dr. Greenspan, I had underlined the last sentence in your statement, as had Senator Graham, so I will read it again. "For the Congress, a crucial focus should be continuing the process of fiscal consolidation and rectifying the secular shortfall in domestic saving that is limiting the growth of our Nation's productivity potential."

And you divided that into two. In the first part you said, well, if we were to undertake actions, even if they did not go into effect until 2005 or 2015 but put them on the books now, that would have an effect on long-term interest rates.

Dr. GREENSPAN. Now.

The CHAIRMAN. We pass it now. It may not go into effect for 10, 12, 15 years, but we pass it now. Are you thinking about something like raising the age on Social Security retirement?

Dr. GREENSPAN. Yes. In fact, one of the recommendations of the Social Security Commission a decade ago was, in fact, to do that. My argument at the time was that, in order to make a sound Social Security system we ought to stabilize the ratio of the number of years in which the average beneficiary receives benefits to the number of years that the beneficiary works and contributes to the fund.

Since life expectancy has been rising, the only way to do that is to index the age of retirement in some manner to life expectancy, preferably at, say, age 60, or something like that.

The CHAIRMAN. That is interesting. I checked those figures, though, and there is a difference. Life expectancy from birth has changed significantly. Once you have made it to 20, life expectancy from 20 onward is not overwhelmingly different between now and when Social Security was founded. Mainly it is because of the success we have had in the decline of death at birth.

Dr. GREENSPAN. I think that is correct in general.

But my impression is that life expectancy at age 60 has been rising.

The CHAIRMAN. But I am with you on changing the age. It has not risen that much.

Dr. GREENSPAN. No. It certainly has not risen as much as the total.

The CHAIRMAN. The total life expectancy.

Dr. GREENSPAN. Sure. Yes.

The CHAIRMAN. Second question. "Rectifying the secular shortfall in domestic savings that is limiting the growth of our Nation's productivity potential." And you indicated, in responding to Senator Graham on that, if we could just narrow the deficit by spending restraints, that would increase our savings potential.

I want to go further and ask you this question. You know the argument. Our Tax Code tilts heavily toward consumption and not nearly enough towards savings and investment. One, is that presumption true?

Dr. GREENSPAN. I am sorry. Would you repeat that?

The CHAIRMAN. Our Tax Code's presumption—and it may or may not be true—tilts more heavily towards consumption than towards savings and investment.

Dr. GREENSPAN. Yes, I think it does.

The CHAIRMAN. Should we attempt to tilt it in the other direction?

Dr. GREENSPAN. I think it would be wise if we did. There are a number of bills which are floating around the Senate which do go in that direction.

The CHAIRMAN. There are a number. Nunn-Domenici is one.

Dr. GREENSPAN. Yes.

The CHAIRMAN. To put it in its simplest terms, it is a gigantic savings exception. You pay a tax on what consume and pay nothing on what you save. That is the simple form. You could do it with a flat tax, if it was low enough.

Dr. GREENSPAN. Yes.

The CHAIRMAN. But you are going to have to make some exceptions for the poor or you are going to have an immense regressivity. That is something Senator Bradley and I, in essence, tried to do, with Senator Moynihan's support, in 1986.

There is a vote in progress. I did not realize that.

Dr. GREENSPAN. Yes, sir.

The CHAIRMAN. I am sorry. Go ahead, Pat.

Senator MOYNIHAN. Could I just say to Dr. Greenspan how much we have enjoyed this? Some day he might come back and talk to us about the subject of whether we really need to have a new equivalent of Breton Woods to look at our international stabilizing systems in the aftermath of a huge change in the world from the time of Breton Woods. That is a subject we might think about.

Dr. GREENSPAN. I think a review of the change in the global financial system specifically as a consequence of the improved telecommunications and computer technology is something which would be a useful subject for evaluation.

Senator MOYNIHAN. Mr. Chairman, thank you.

The CHAIRMAN. Dr. Greenspan, thank you very much for coming. I am sure you will be back.

Dr. GREENSPAN. Thank you.

Senator MOYNIHAN. Thank you, sir.

[Whereupon, at 12:02 p.m., the hearing was adjourned.]

APPENDIX

Additional Material Submitted

Prepared Statement of Alan Greenspan

Mr. Chairman, members of the Committee, I am pleased to be able to appear here today, to offer my thoughts on the economic backdrop for your policy discussions.

The U.S. economy has recorded some notable achievements over the past few years, but there is nonetheless much left to be accomplished. The fiscal decisions made by the Congress in the next several months will play a critical role in determining the economic welfare of our citizens over the years—indeed, the decades—to come.

I perhaps should begin with a brief review of the current condition of the economy. There is no question that the past year was one of remarkable progress along many dimensions of macroeconomic performance. The official estimates for the fourth quarter are not yet available, but it is clear that real gross domestic product expanded by about four percent over the course of 1994—the best gain in some time, and one that surpassed most expectations. Importantly, we saw an accelerated expansion of employment as well. Cumulatively, payrolls have now increased roughly 6 million over the past couple of years, belying in dramatic fashion the notion that had developed earlier in this decade that our economy had lost its job-generating ability. With the rapid growth of employment, the national unemployment rate has fallen sharply, to less than 5½ percent this past month.

The economic gains have been broad. They have encompassed almost all major segments of industry and all parts of the country. The expansion in recent quarters has been paced by growth of business investment and exports, and as a consequence, we have seen not only a continuation of robust increases in service sector employment but also a significant upturn in job creation in the manufacturing sector. Manufacturing output increased 6.8 percent last year, and *measured* factory employment rose almost 300,000, I say "measured" because it has been true for some time now that manufacturers have relied to an increasing degree on workers supplied by temporary help firms, which are recorded separately in the service industry. But it is clear that last year saw a significant gain in the overall factory workforce. Moreover, I would note the reports in the recent "Beige Book" survey assembled by our regional Reserve Banks that manufacturers now are expressing a greater inclination to add workers directly to their payrolls. This is a sign of the greater confidence that firms now have that future levels of activity will remain high.

Geographically, contractions in some sectors such as defense and finance have left their negative imprint on certain locales, but rising activity and improving job opportunities have characterized most areas of the country. Notably, California—accounting for roughly an eighth of the nation's economy—appears to be in the process of turning around. Unemployment rates have fallen in all regions, and are lower in most now than they were at the peak of the last business cycle expansion. Moreover, the gains in employment have benefited all major demographic segments of the labor force as well.

Of crucial importance to the sustainability of these gains, they have been achieved without a deterioration in the overall inflation rate. The Consumer Price Index rose 2.7 percent last year, the same as in 1993. Inflation at the retail level, as measured by the CPI, has been a bit less than 3 percent for three years running now—the first time that has occurred since the early 1960s. This is a signal accomplishment, for it marks a move toward a more stable economic environment in which households, businesses, and governmental units can plan with greater confidence and operate with greater efficiency. When we consider the probable upward bias of the

CPI, it would appear that we have gotten close to achieving effective price stability, though we're not there yet.

In 1994, we had a difficult reversal in monetary policy to navigate. The overhang of debt and the strains that emerged among our financial intermediaries, especially out of the commercial real estate collapse of the late 1980s, required a heavy dose of monetary ease beginning in 1989 to alleviate a significant credit crunch. The danger of overstaying that policy of ease was clear, particularly as we moved through 1993, but the right time to change course was difficult to determine. Judging from the developments of the past year, it appears that our policy reversal last February was timely—but we won't know for sure except in retrospect.

As I have stated many times in Congressional testimony, I believe firmly that a key ingredient in achieving the highest possible levels of productivity, real incomes, and living standards is the achievement of price stability. Thus, I see it as crucial that we extend the recent trend of low and, hopefully, declining inflation in the years ahead. The prospects in this regard are fundamentally good, but there are reasons for some concern, at least with respect to the nearer term. Those concerns relate primarily to the fact that resource utilization rates already have risen to high levels by recent historical standards. The current unemployment rate, for example, is comparable to the average of the late 1980s, when wages and prices accelerated appreciably. The same is true of the capacity utilization rate in the industrial sector.

Clearly, one factor in judging the inflationary risks in the economy is the potential for expansion of our productive capacity. If "potential GDP" is growing rapidly, actual output can also continue to grow rapidly without intensifying pressures on resources. In this regard, many commentators, myself included, have remarked that there is something of a more-than-cyclical character to the evident improvement of America's competitive capabilities in recent years. Our dominance in computer software, for example, has moved us back to a position of clear leadership in advanced technology after some faltering in the 1970s. But, while most analysts have increased their estimates of America's long-term productivity growth, it is still too soon to judge whether that improvement is a few tenths of a percentage point annually, or even more, perhaps moving us much closer to the more vibrant pace that characterized the early post-World War II period. It is fair to note, however, that the fact that labor and factory utilization rates have risen as much as they have in the past year or so does argue that the rate of increase in potential is appreciably below the 4 percent growth rate of 1994.

Knowing in advance our true growth potential obviously would be useful in setting policy, because history tells us that economies that strain labor force and capital stock limits tend to engender inflationary instabilities which undermine growth. Moreover, in such an environment asset prices can begin to rise unsustainably, contributing to an unstable financial and economic environment. It is true, however, that in modern economies output levels may not be so rigidly constrained in the short run as they used to be when large segments of output were governed by facilities such as the old open hearth steel furnaces that had rated capacities that could not be exceeded for long without breakdown. Rather, the appropriate analogy is a flexible ceiling that can be stretched when pressed; but, as the degree of pressure increases, the extent of flexibility diminishes. It is possible for the economy to exceed "potential" for a time without adverse consequences by extending workhours, by deferring maintenance, and by forgoing longer-term projects. Moreover, as world trade expands, access to foreign sources of supply augments to a degree the flexibility of domestic productive facilities for goods and some services.

Aggregative indicators, such as the unemployment rate and capacity utilization, may be suggestive of emerging inflation and asset price instability problems. But, they cannot be determinative. History shows clearly that given levels of resource utilization can be associated with a wide range of inflation rates. Accordingly, policymakers must monitor developments on an ongoing basis to gauge when economic potential actually is beginning to become strained—irrespective of where current unemployment rates or capacity utilization rates may lie. If we are endeavoring to fend off instability before it becomes debilitating to economic growth, direct evidence of the emerging process is essential. Consequently, one must look beyond broad indicators to gauge the inflationary tendencies in the economy.

In this context, aggregate measures of pressure in labor and product markets do seem to be validated by finer statistical and anecdotal indications of tensions. In the manufacturing sector, for example, purchasing managers report slower supplier deliveries and increasing shortages of materials. Indeed, firms appear to have been building their inventories of materials in recent months so as to ensure that they will have adequate supplies on hand to meet their production schedules. These pressures have been mirrored in a sharp rise over the past year in the prices of raw materials and intermediate components. There are increasing reports that firms are considering marking up the prices of final goods to offset those increased costs. In the labor market, anecdotal reports of "shortages" of workers have become more common—as indicated, for example, in our Beige Book last week—and there are vague signs of upward pressures on wages. To be sure, increased wages are a good thing if they can be achieved without commensurate acceleration in prices, but they are not beneficial if they are merely a part of a general pickup in inflation. A hopeful sign in this regard, however, is that to date the trends in money and credit expansion have remained subdued. They do not suggest that what I've referred to elsewhere as the "financial tinder" needed to support on ongoing inflation process is in place.

That kind of ongoing process also would be expected to involve a different expectational climate than seems to prevail today. Despite the marked improvement in consumer confidence overall, the survey readings on consumers' views of whether jobs are easy to get fall far short of the previous cyclical peak in 1989. Moreover, there is evidence that the number of people voluntarily leaving their jobs is subnormal currently. This suggests that the deep-seated fear of job insecurity has not fully dissipated despite ample evidence of strong job growth recently.

Some analysts attribute this phenomenon to workers' concerns about losing health insurance and, for some, pension coverage if they change jobs. Whatever the cause, the lingering sense of insecurity doubtless has been a factor damping wage growth and overall labor costs. Since the latter, on a consolidated basis, account for roughly two-thirds of overall costs in our economy, slower wage growth combined with strong cyclical productivity growth has restrained increases in unit labor costs and hence in prices of final goods and services.

However, as overall output growth of necessity slows in an environment of high resource utilization, so will cyclical productivity growth. Moreover, if labor market tightness assuages fears of job insecurity, pressures to raise wages will intensify and unit labor costs could accelerate. In the later stages of previous business cycles, profit margins were squeezed, but some of the underlying unit labor cost increases were nonetheless passed through into final goods prices and inflation picked up. Thus far in the current cycle, any tendency toward the emergence of this kind of process has been muted by a prevailing concern among firms that, despite capacity pressures, enough slack and subdued unit costs remain in the system to foster competitive inroads on those who try to price above the market. But this form of discipline may also become less effective as pressures on resources persist. Consequently, it may be that these pressures will lead to some deterioration in the price picture in the near term; but any such deterioration should be contained if the Federal Reserve remains vigilant.

The actions of the Congress and the Administration in the fiscal sphere will also be important in maintaining public confidence that inflation will be subdued. There can be no doubt that the persistence of large federal budget deficits represents in the minds of many individuals a potential risk. While we clearly have avoided it in recent years, history is replete with examples of fiscal pressures leading to monetary excesses and then to greater inflation. Currently, I strongly suspect that investors here and abroad are exacting from issuers of dollar-denominated debt an extra inflation risk premium that reflects not their estimate of the most likely rate of price level increase over the life of the obligation, but the possibility that it could prove to be significantly greater. This inflation risk premium is costly, because it raises the hurdle that must be surpassed when looking at the expected returns on possible investment projects.

But the influence of the fiscal imbalance of the federal government on capital formation is broader than that. The federal deficit drains off a large share of a regrettably small pool of domestic private saving, thus contributing further—and perhaps to an even greater degree—to the elevation of real rates of interest in the economy. Admittedly, there is some uncertainty about the causes of what seem to be relatively high real long-term rates around the world, as was noted by leaders of the largest industrial nations at their summit meeting last year. But the vast majority of analysts would agree that in the United States the current sizable federal deficits, and the projected growth of those deficits over the decades ahead, are a significant element in the story.

In sum, the recent performance of the macroeconomy has been encouraging. But much of the improvement is in the nature of cyclical developments and we all have our work cut out for us if we are to extend these gains and foster long-term trends that enhance the welfare of all of our citizens. The central role of the Federal Reserve today is to ensure that our economy remains on a sustainable, noninflationary path. For the Congress, a crucial focus should be continuing the process of fiscal consolidation and rectifying the secular shortfall in domestic saving that is limiting the growth of our nation's productive potential.

O

88-545 (40)